THE
FORENSIC
PSYCHOLOGY
OF
THEFT,
BURGLARY
AND
PROPERTY CRIME:

CONNOR WHITELEY

ACKNOWLEDGMENTS

Thank you to all my readers without you I couldn't do what I love.

INTRODUCTION

Forensic psychology has to be one of my favourite areas of psychology. It tells us why people commit crimes, how to treat them and how to reduce the chance of them committing the offence again.

So, whilst this book won't be talking about the very board reach of Forensic Psychology, please know the author of this book is extremely passionate about this area!

<u>What is This Book About?</u>

Following the release of my main Forensic Psychology book, a lot of readers wanted me to write more about forensic psychology. So, I decided to write some shorter forensic psychology books.

This is the first of a few shorter books I plan to write. Therefore, this book is all about the psychology of theft, burglary, and other types of property crime. Including arson and pyromania. (I really enjoy that chapter!)

Including the causes, is there such thing as a criminal expert and how burglars make decisions about what to steal and more.

Who Is This Book For?

Whether you're a psychology student, a trained professional wanting to learn more, or a person just interested in forensic psychology. Then this is the book for you!

Especially, if you want an engaging book that explains everything in an easy-to-understand way.

I never write my books like a boring dry academic textbook. So, please do not expect this book to be one.

Instead, look forward to reading a book about forensic psychology that's interesting and explains information in an easy-to-understand way. Without all the complex jargon.

Or better yet, imagine this book as sitting down with a friend for a conversation about forensic psychology.

Who Am I?

As a reader, I always have to know that the nonfiction book, I'm reading comes from a person who knows what they're talking about. I hate it when I want to buy a book about psychology only to find it was written by someone who never went to university.

In case, you're like me, I'm Connor Whiteley an author of over 10 psychology books and I'm the host of the weekly The Psychology World Podcast available on all major podcast apps. Here, I talk about a different psychology topic each week and soon we'll reach our 100th episode!

Also, I'm a psychology student at the University of Kent, England and in 2021/ 2022, I'll be working with a team of psychology researchers during my placement.

So, now the introduction is over, let's get into the forensic psychology of theft and property crime!

CHAPTER 1: THEFT AND
SHOPLIFTING

I know we would start this forensic psychology book by looking at theft, because whilst historically, forensic psychology has ignored this area of crime. Since psychological factors seemed to be only marginally relevant. (McGuire, 2004) Theft is still extremely important to look at. Especially, when we consider how common it is compared to other types of crime.

You can define theft as basically taking something that doesn't belong to you without permission from the owner. And we need to look at this type of crime because in society it has sort of become normalised to varying degrees.

By this I mean, it is basically normal to keep the change after your caregivers give you £5 to go and buy something that costs £4.75. I know it says silly but that keeping that 25 pence without permission is still theft.

If people were charged for that I would be on a life sentence by now!

Another normal example is piracy. Whether it's music, films or books, this is sadly common and as an author. This does sadden me because if someone pirates my books then I don't get the money, and I can't make a living.

But this is still very common.

To further emphasise my point, Budd, Sharp and Mayhew (2005) conducted a study to see how common theft is in society. Their results show an interesting picture.

For example, 40% of males and 22% of females were reported to have committed a property crime.

Another finding was 35% of men and 1% of women had admitted to minor theft. Like, theft from school or work. (I may have *borrowed* some things from school in the past)

In addition, 11% of men and 2% of women have committed vehicle theft in the past.

Finally, the study found theft from people compared to other settings, like school, work amongst others, were very common. With less than 1% of men and less than 0.5% of women thieving from people.

Overall, I think this greatly shows that whilst theft is relatively common. The idea of your home WILL be a target for criminals might be a great marketing tactic from home security companies. (But still better safe than sorry)

Motivations:

With theft being relatively common, why do people do it?

Of course, there is no one answer to this question but throughout the book, we'll be looking into this in more depth.

One study that aims to answer this question is Steinmetz and Tunnel (2013) who found thieves tend to have the following motivations, and I should note all these motivations tend to apply to pirates- the people who pirate books, music and films.

Firstly, they have the desire to share content with people. This I can understand but again it does have a real impact on people's livelihoods. And from a psychological perspective, this might be more of a tactic to maintain positive self-image compared to the genuine desire to share content with people.

Secondly, people want to listen to something

before they buy it. A good idea perhaps, but would they buy it when they can listen to it for free?

Another motivation is to get unaffordable content. This I completely understand because I have been tempted to do the same because I will never buy a £30 eBook. I didn't get the pirate copy but I understand.

A final motivation is thieves have a subversive wish to undermine copyright law and the music industry who makes unjustifiable profits.

Personally, I don't completely understand this motivation but that could be because I understand and love copyright law. Since it's these laws that allow me to make money.

Shoplifting:

Moving onto a more focused area of theft, shoplifting is when a person takes something from a shop without paying for it. That's a simple definition.

Also, I remember back when I was about 8 years olds and a police officer came into our school. To tell us that shoplifting was bad, and it was so common, it didn't even get reported on the news.

Referring to a more official source, according to Hopkins (2002) 80% of retailers and 63% of manufacturers experienced a crime compared to only

30% of people. As well as alcoholic drinking shops and DIY stores are more likely to be burglarized.

Overall, shoplifting is surprisingly common.

Situational Action Theory

There have been a lot of theories that try to explain why theft and shoplifting occurs. Therefore, we need to look at Situational Action Theory (SAT) because it combines environmental explanations with psychological explanations to explain why this type of offending occurs.

To see how the theory works Hirtenlehnera and Hardie (2016) used it to explain adolescent shoplifting. With the theory bringing together a person's mortality, environmental factor, self-control, and social control (deterrents) to predict whether a person will shoplift.

The theory proposes that when our mortality and the social controls are criminogenic (right for crime), we commit crime.

For example, if a person didn't see shoplifting as bad and there were no members of staff or cameras about. This would make the situation right for committing a crime. Thus, the person probably would commit the shoplifting offence.

Shoplifter Tactics to Avoid Getting Caught:

Shoplifters use a lot of tactics to avoid getting caught and arrested. As I was reading the research in this area, I was rather entertained by how crafty and clever some of the offenders were. And please don't try these at home! (or in shops!)

The main tactic we'll look at in the book is from Laskey, Jacques and Fisher (2005) when they found the most common tactic for shoplifting is blending in with other shoppers.

At first, this might sound simple and boring, but this isn't as straightforward as you might think. Since the shoplifter needs to employ a mental schema, deeply rooted mental representations or frameworks that affect how we encode, store and retrieve information, about how normal shoppers speak, act and communication based on their own normal experience.

Additionally, the researchers interviewed shoplifters and the offenders said shoplifting happens in three stages.

Firstly, they enter the shop to find an item to steal, and they show signs of being a normal shopper by getting another trolley and they examine other items.

Next, the shoplifter takes the item. A clever

way of doing this was to use a phone and hold it close to the object. Before taking both the phone and the object away at the same time.

Then stage 3 is leaving the shop in a normal manner to avoid drawing suspicion.

On a more practical note, these tactics make it difficult for security to catch the shoplifters. Especially, when the shoplifters merge into large groups of people.

One way to deal with this problem is to look out for a particular type of person but if arrests are systemically biased. Then looking for a particular type of person will reproduce the bias, and could be considered oppressive.

I certainly agree with the previous point because whenever I would go into certain shops between the ages of 17 to 19. I would always be stopped on the way out even if I was out with my dad shopping. Since because I was of the age where I was likely to shoplift.

Personally, I never would shoplift!

This was disgraceful I think, and this is another reason why I support the Black Lives Matter movement. When people were saying that black people getting pulled over more isn't biased.

It clearly is. especially, when I keep getting stopped in shops because I'm the age where I'm likely to shoplift.

Shop Workers:

It should be noted though that it isn't only customers stealing from shops. Workers can steal from their employers too. With something in excess of over half of shopworkers stealing something from their workplace in the past. (Winbush and Datton, 1997) Leading to this costing the US economy $40 million each year.

Furthermore, I know it's a common thought that this happens because employees are dissatisfied with their employers. And it's true some dissatisfied employees do steal. This is a logical thought but there are still plenty of employees that don't steal.

Although, there is an interesting way to prevent this workplace theft. As a result after looking at age, whistleblowing climate and stock shrinkage theft due to staff. Avery, McKay and Hunter (2012) found stores employing older staff members experienced less shrinkage.

What makes this interesting is it seems these older members of staff seem to be guardians against theft from other members.

This effect can even be increased if the

environment in the shop isn't criminogenic.

This is further supported by Kulas et al (2007) who argues theft is more likely in organisations where the environment the employees are in are conducive to theft.

Typically, these are organisations where it is easy to steal because staff members perceive other peers as committing crimes, they're likely not to get caught and co-workers are permissive about theft.

However, we all know stealing is bad and this can cause us to feel bad about it later.

Consequently, in all these situations, people used several tactics to make themselves feel better. These are tactics or verbal devices used to justify the theft, avoid self-blame, and maintain positive self-image.

These tactics include their economic need, like I need the money to help pay my bills, limiting the extent of theft, like I'll only steal once, and deserving the money. as well as having a no one cares attitude.

CHAPTER 2: BURGLARY: TYPES OF BULGARS, THE BURGLARY -DRUG CONNECTION AND DECISION-MAKING PROCESSES

I really couldn't look at property crime without looking at burglaries, because whenever we think about property crime, this is the top of my list. Before researching this topic, I had no idea shoplifting counted as a type of property crime.

Like all areas of psychology, forensic psychology likes to categorise people into different types, understandingly. However, forensic psychology has typically failed to find types of burglars using qualitative methods.

Nonetheless, this didn't stop Vaughan, De Lisi, Breaver and Howard (2008) from trying to research this area by choosing a quantitative approach by interviewing 550 career criminals.

Personally, I want to say well done them. That's a lot of data to collect and analyse!

In addition, the information from the interviews were supplemented by official records.

Interestingly, this study made use of an extremely unusual feature since the researchers were working for a bail bond company, this information was collected under oath. This is massive for their data because it means it's extremely likely to be reliable and this minimizes the social desirability bias.

Furthermore, their results showed there are different types of burglars. For example, there are versatile burglars. These tend to be young offenders with different types of crimes on their criminal records.

Another type of burglar is the vagrant burglar. These offenders tend to be charged with numerous crimes, which are the primary consequence of their vagrant lifestyle. With these offenders committing the burglaries for material gain and to ensure they survive the winter months.

And in case you're like me who doesn't know what the word *vagrant* means. It means a person who doesn't have a permeant home and travels from place to place.

The third type of burglar is the drug-oriented

burglar. These offenders have a number of background offences including drug possession and trafficking. As well as they often have a lot of theft and weapon charges. Typically, these offenders use their crimes to pay for the drugs, and they use aliases and were tattooed.

Moreover, the final type of burglar is the sex predator burglar. Typically, this is showed by signs of the involvement of deviant sexual acts. Also, their crime history is likely to include rapes and position offences. Overall, this group of burglars were the most violent and had the longest-lasting criminal histories. Which tended to start in childhood.

Now, I must mention if you've done forensic psychology before or if you've read a book on it. You might be questioning how valid typologies are, and I completely agree. Sometimes they are questionable.

However, in this case, such a typology is useful since it suggests there are several routines for burglars to commit their crimes. This provides a basis for further research. As well as the identification of a drug-oriented group is important given the strong connection between drug use and acquisitive crimes.

Burglary- drug connection

Leading on from the last topic, I think this borders on the stereotype because I can think of several TV programmes that make great use of drug addicts breaking into people's houses. In an effort to fun their addiction or to help pay off their drug debts.

Of course, as with most things in the TV world, this might be based on a little bit of truth but then it's blown out of portion. Since it is correct that some burglars do steal for drug money but not all. And that's the focus of this section.

Therefore, as I've already said not all burglar use drugs but there does seem to be a connection between burglars and drugs.

Forensic psychology tends to think this connection has 3 bases or reasons. The first is drug users tend to associate more with criminals which may lead to a greater involvement in crime. This makes sense because it links into social influence in Social Psychology.

Another base for this connection is drugs are expensive and not all drug users can finance them through legitimate means. Like, a day job. So, burglary can help pay for the drugs on top of their day job. But most drug users do use legitimate means.

The other base of this connection is the idea

that a third factor could influence the drug and burglary connection separately. For example, inadequate parenting could lead to criminality and drug use separately. If you're familiar with correlational research then this is basically the third variable problem.

Equally, another factor influencing this connection is the drugs could have pharmacological effects which lead to the offending. (Bureau of Justice Stats, 2013)

Overall, there is plenty of evidence to show a relationship between drug use and property crime. Yet finding evidence of the drug use causes the burglary (or vice versa) and proving this is a causal relationship is hard.

To finish up this section, according to the Home Office (2002) over half of all crimes in the UK are committed by drug users. And this is even higher for shoplifting at 85% and domestic burglary.

Although, if this is a causal relationship then you might except property crime to fluctuate as the price of drugs does. For example, when the price of drugs decreases, the rate of property crime decrease as the burglars don't need to commit as many crimes to afford the drugs.

Interestingly, this is supported by Degenhardt

et al (2005) when there was a sudden change in the availability of heroin in Australia and the rate of property crime changed accordingly.

Burglar Decision Making:

If you broke into a house, what would you take? Small items? Big items? Jewellery? Or where would you search first? Bedroom? Kitchen? Living room?

I know this sounds weird to ask but these are the sort of questions that constantly go around in a burglar's head. They have precious time to make these decisions, grab the goods and go.

This is even harder when you consider that the house, they're in is unfamiliar to them and the naïve burglar is likely to be fixated. Whereas most experienced burglars know what to grab and where it is kept.

So, this leads to the question: how do burglars decide what to take?

Thankfully, there are several theories to help us answer this question.

Routine Activity Theory:

This theory emphasises it is the day-to-day activities of people and the structure of their daily lives that provides them with the opportunity to commit crimes.

Immediately, I have to admit this is interesting because it means we basically live our lives in a way that allows us to commit crimes.

In support of the theory, Felson (1996) identified 3 factors that contribute to property crime showing how the offender's lifestyle contributes to the crime.

Firstly, motivated offenders tend to commit crimes in their local area. There is some variance to this point but I'll explain that later.

Secondly, suitable properties in the local area tend to be an attractive target for a potential burglar.

Lastly, there is an absence of guardians to protect the property. In my opinion, I think the terms guardian is strange as I imagine knights in shiny armour standing outside the property.

In reality, this means there is a lack of social guardians. (Johnson and Bowers, 2004) These are presences like people who protect the property. This can be as simple as you being home. Typically, this is the reason why most offenders avoid occupied places. As well as there are physical guardians like CCTV cameras.

What Makes a Suitable Property?

Of course, there is no perfect property that will certainly be targeted by a burglar. However, there are factors that can increase the chance of getting burglarized.

Additionally, all these factors and more play into the burglar's decision making processes and the assessment of the property when choosing whether to strike or not.

For example, if a property has a greater value as judged by the burglar. Then this will naturally be more interesting to them.

Another factor is the lack of physical characteristics that increase the risk of offending. For instance, security cameras increases the risk because they're more likely to be caught. Unless they deal with the cameras!

In addition, a suitable property for burglars is a property that lacks other people seeing it. Meaning if you have a house surrounded by tall houses, this makes it difficult for neighbours or passers-by to see inside. This decreases the chance of them seeing the burglars break in.

Bringing in specific research support, Nee and Meenaghan (2006) found that over 75% of burglars prefer unoccupied homes and they check the property is empty before breaking in.

However, as we can all probably guess this assessment isn't always successful. Leading to the burglar sometimes resulting to acts of violence or opportunistic sex crimes when they get caught. And this failed assessment increases the risk of getting arresting.

Testing It All

So far in this burglar decision-making section, we've spoken a lot about the different factors that burglars consider. But is it all accurate in the real world?

Therefore, Tseloni, Witterbrood, Farrel and Pease (2004) wanted to test this theory in the USA, England, Wales and the Netherlands. Their results showed several interesting findings. For instance, as expected properties with fewer social guardians increased the risk of burglary.

Another surprising finding was households that had preventive measures were more likely to be burglarized. Now, I have to admit this is very surprising and concerning. Yet this is unclear and could be down to the homeowner's half-hearted preventive measures. Like, using a fake security camera or a house alarm that doesn't actually work.

I know the last one sounds like I'm making it up but I've seen casings for home alarms you can buy and attach to your house. So, it looks like your house is wired to a security company but in reality, it's an empty plastic box with an LED light on it. Making potential burglars think it works.

The last finding was living in the inner city or urbanised areas increased the risk of burglary. This could be because these properties are closer to where the offenders live.

Although, when the data was looked into in more depth, the relationship between the theory and the data wasn't complete and it left a lot to be explained.

Rational Choice Theory:

This theory has been labelled possibly the most important alternative to ideas about personal propensity to commit crimes. Since it proposes offenders seek an advantage for themselves using meanings that are rational within the constraints of the information available to them, the offender's reasoning ability and time available.

Taking a step back, instead of this theory saying the person committed the crime because they have criminal tendencies. This theory is saying the person committed the crime because it is a rational choice given the information available to them.

Moreover, the theory acknowledges other factors play a role in criminality. Like, drunkenness, having a row as well as poor upbringing.

Pease (2001) said this theory freed researcher from having to looking to the pathological characteristics of offenders.

This is a positive for researchers because if you've read my main Forensic Psychology book then you'll know a lot of criminals have nothing pathological about them. as far as society is concerned, they're *normal*.

Also, research has shown burglars are far less opportunistic as once thought. Which makes sense because everything already mentioned in this section shows several cognitive processes occur when burglars are deciding which property to burgle.

According to Snook, Dhami and Kavangh (2011) the rational choice model proposes criminals only makes rational decisions. They do a cost-benefit analysis.

Nevertheless, this theory isn't perfect because researchers have questioned if the theory is right about burglars using cool, cognitive processing.

In my opinion, I do agree with this argument

because I can imagine that not all burglars always use cold calculative thinking when planning a burglary.

For example, based on good evidence, Shower and Hocheter (2002) didn't believe burglars were as calculating as the model believed.

Leading to Van Gelder (2013) to propose a two process 'hot-cool- model where both 'cool' cognitive processing and 'hot' affective feelings influence the offender.

I think we can agree Van Gelder's idea is probably more accurate when you consider the research done in Social Psychology and Cognitive Psychology. In terms of how emotions can impact our decision making amongst other cognitive processes.

Nonetheless, the theory is still interesting to consider and as Pease (2001) mentioned this freed researchers to look at other angles. And this is the great thing about psychology, we always need to be advancing the field and questioning what we know at the time.

CHAPTER 3: EXPERTISE IN CRIME

When I first read this topic, I was rather interested because the idea of some criminals being better or more effective than others isn't new. But to learn what the psychology literature had to say about it was very interesting. Especially when it comes to burglars.

Consequently, it isn't surprising after reading the last chapter that burglars have a range of complex cognitive processes available to them. This has many benefits for them. like, burglars, especially experienced ones, could largely be on autopilot once inside.

The main reason for this is because burglars rely a lot on schemas. These are deeply rooted mental representations or frameworks that affect how we encode, store and retrieve information.

Also, it isn't surprising to know that burglars

vary in skill a lot. For example, the stereotypical dumb burglar and the charming suited jewel thief ideas from TV could be considered accurate here.

According to the research, 'expert' burglars (Clare, 2011) had better domain-specific burglary skills. Meaning they were better in their burglary skills than non-experts.

As well as they showed generally homogenous (consistent) patterns when selecting and searching property by operating largely in an automatic manner. This into other research that shows burglars often repeat themselves so burglars hit same types of homes as other successful offences. (Pease, 1998)

Although another key difference is that expert burglars were able to deal with large amounts of information quickly and effectively.

However, if we start to think about what makes an expert burglar then it's useful to think about differences. For example, expert burglars tend to start younger than novices, their first burglary was more likely to involve other offenders as well as expert burglars are less afraid of being arrested. Also, experts are more willing and likely to travel further to commit their crimes.

Whereas novice burglars are more likely to burgle acquisitively. Another term for personal gain.

As well as the novices are more likely to be detected by different targets.

Other Crimes:

Whilst expertise in burglary is well-research, it's hardly the only type of crime to show elements of expertise. For instance, carjacking is another. (Topalli, Jacques and Wright, 2015)

The main reason for this is because there are two aspects of expertise in carjacking. Firstly, there's the value of the car and the other aspect is the commandeering. Since the more expensive cars tend to have more security features and are harder to commandeer.

While we're talking about commandeering, it should be mentioned that some carjackers avoid female victims because they're more likely to scream. Whereas other carjackers prefer to target them because women are typically less likely to win a physical confrontation.

In addition, in carjacking and other types of crime, these involve a mental script. This is a part of our cognition that tells us exactly what to do in a given situation.

Expertise on the Whole:

Overall, expertise is a continuum where criminals can progress and improve.

This thinking prompted Nee and Ward (2015) to propose the following from basic research and they developed their difunctional expertise model.

The first part of their model was called 'Chunking'. This is where through the process of trial and error a novice criminal starts to understand what factors lead to successful outcomes. As well as what factors lead to negative outcomes. These pieces of information become chunks and these can be recalled quickly as problems arise. Also, as the novice uses these chunks will become schemas over time.

The second part of the model was automaticity. Basically when the behaviours become automatic to the novice offender.

In addition, cognitive research shows this automaticity doesn't take hundreds of repetitions to develop like previously thought.

Situational Awareness and Selective Preconscious:

Expert criminals and offenders are skilled at attending to, storing and recalling information that might be used to make future decisions. Meaning they're better able to evaluate what's happening around them compared to novices.

Which as you can guess becomes very useful in the future to become more effective and avoid getting arrested.

<u>Multi-Taking:</u>

This type of cognitive process involves automatic, highly learned, unconscious decision-making processes that takes little cognitive effort for the expert burglar. Resulting in the burglar being able to think about other things and listen out for signs of danger. Compared to a novice who needs to make fresh decisions at every turn.

The concept of multi-tasking was supported by Nee (2015) who found burglars tend to search the master bedroom first, the other adult bedrooms then a quick search of downstairs bedrooms. With expert burglars going for smaller items and they avoided more identifiable ones. Like, china, silver and artwork.

However, the idea of expertise is only illustrative. Since no research shows how expertise is learnt. Meaning this concept only has limited real-world use.

But it's still interesting and still shows the cognitive, practical and social skills involved in crime.

CHAPTER 4: ARSON AND PYROMANIA

So far in the book, we've looked at theft, shoplifting, burglary and expertise. However, no one can talk about property crime and not discuss arson. Especially, with TV programmes and films making great use of this type of crime.

Consequently, many arsonists are from impoverished homes as well as they tend to have histories of antisocial behaviour from childhood onwards. (Harley and Bowlby, 2011)

In terms of motivations, most firesetters are motivated by money, revenge, or retribution. (Punishment)

Thankfully, UK statistics show a very clear decreasing trend in deliberate fire setting. (Home Office, 2016c) With the number of fires decreasing overall due to innovations. Like, fire-resistant furniture.

In addition, according to the UK's Government's Crime Reduction Toolkit (Home Office, 2005a) For Arson, the major reasons for the firesetting behaviour can be broken down in the following ways. For instance, about 5% of arson are malicious with them being motivated by racism and revenge.

Another 5% of arson cases are psychological in nature being set due to mental conditions or suicidal attempts.

The third major reason is criminal where the arsonist lights the to conceal a crime or when a person may profit from fire. Such as in cases of Insurance fraud.

Finally, the most common reason for fire setting is youth disorder and nuisance. Making up 80% of arson cases. Also, boredom and thrill-seeking may be associated with this particular reason.

As a result, it isn't exactly surprising to learn that males under 18 years old make up over half of offenders for arson. As well as roughly a third of US arson offenders are under 15 years old. (Hickle and Roe-Sepouitz, 2010)

Meaning as the research suggests many fire setters start their firesetting behaviour early on in life. Suggesting delinquent behaviour plays more a role in fire setting than any deep psychological difficulties. Of course, we're talking about overall here.

<u>Why Commit Arson?</u>

Whilst this is the main focus for the chapter, Almond, Duggan, Shine and Canter (2005)'s study is a good place to start because these researchers investigated Shye's (1985) Action System Model. With their results showing four different 'models' of arson emerging.

Firstly, there is the adaptive model. Which proposes fire setting is caused when an external event is exploited for some sort of gain. Like, burning a crime scene. Since this links to other crimes, this type of arson can be linked to vehicle theft amongst others.

Secondly, there is the expressive model where the arsonist uses the fire as a way to express internal psychological factors against the target of the arson. This could include venting your anger at a shop that kicked you out for something you didn't do.

The third model is called the Integrative model where internal psychological factors are dealt with by using arson as a means of seeking attention. This model even includes setting themselves a light to gain attention.

Lastly, the researchers found the conservative model where an external source of frustration leads to the person to set a fire to restore their well-being. For example, using arson to get revenge on someone or something.

Nevertheless, no piece of research is perfect and a critical point of this study is it only uses convicted arsonists and not a sample of the whole fire setting population.

Female Arsonists

Generally, females are underrepresented in the fire setting literature. However, when Gannon (2010) reviewed the literature, she found that females arsonists were less likely to watch the consequences of their fire. Like, the firefighting efforts. As well as female arsonists showed a higher prevalence of depression and psychosis than male arsonists.

Additionally, female arsonists didn't show sexual fetishism involving fire nor did they typically carry out arson for profit or concealment of another crime.

In terms of causes, sexual abuse is more common in the childhoods of female arsonists with various forms of attention-seeking and cries for help being the predominate motivations of female arsonists.

Although, the common causes were found to be very similar for boys and girls. Including abuse, parental absence, absent fathers, child's behaviour poorly monitored by parents, parent lack of affection for child and parents not greatly involved in their children's lives.

I think this highlights the importance of parenting and being there for their child and being a caring caregiver.

Pyromaniacs

I can almost guarantee that some of you were flicking through the pages of this chapter to see when I was going to get to this section. Because let's face it, pyromaniacs are interesting and whenever you see one on TV programmes they are probably one of the most interesting types of offenders. Meaning we had to look at them in this book!

Therefore, one popular view is fires are caused by people who get pleasure from it. (Doley, 2003) These people could be considered pyromaniacs. People who could have an irresistible attraction and even get sexual gratification from fire. This overtime leads to more and more fire setting so the offender can get more sexual gratification.

To become classed as a pyromaniac, a person needs to become diagnosed because pyromania is a mental condition and between the Diagnostic and Statical Manual (DSM) Version 4 and 5, the criterion for diagnosis hasn't changed.

Meaning, for a person to become diagnosed they would have to set a fire deliberately and purposefully on two or more separate occasions. As well as experience a state of emotional tension or arousal before setting the fire.

Furthermore, they would have to have a fascination with or curiosity about fire and the content of fire. Like, the aftermath, how quickly the fire spreads, what's the best fuel to use amongst other things. (Yes, I watch TV)

Also, the person would get a feeling of pleasure or relief when starting a fire or in the aftermath. As well as there shouldn't be any other way to account for the behaviour. Such as a personality or antisocial disorder.

The Truth:

In all honesty, despite TV and films having us believe all arsonists love fire and they're all pyromaniacs. The truth is pyromaniacs seem rare amongst arsonists. (Doley, 2003) And even the idea that all arsonists have a mental condition is wrong. Since only 17% of arsonists have a mental condition. (Almond et al, 2005)

The truth is the idea of pyromaniacs and sexual urges is old and has no research support. As supported by Lewis and Yarnell (1951) who found out of 1100 arsonists only 3% reported sexual urges.

So, I'm sorry if I've busted anyone's ideas about arsonists but sometimes TV just gets it wrong. I talk more about this in my main Forensic Psychology book if you're interested.

Relation to Fire

We all relate to different things in different ways. For example, I relate to books in terms of their characters and plots but their structure and writing techniques. (Real writing techniques, not the rubbish English teachers teach you) I can guarantee that isn't how you relate to books.

Hence, showing how different people relate to things in different ways and fire setting is no different.

As a result of research has found fire setters relate differently to fire to non-fire setters. (O'Ciarrlra, Bornoue, Alleyne, Tyler, Mocova and Gannon, 2015)

For instance, they differ in terms of their identification with fire because fire setters tend to say something like *Fire is a part of me.* Whereas you and I might say we like fire because it keeps us warm.

A second difference is around fire safety since

fire setters might ignore it completely or have their own version of fire safety. Whereas we've likely to follow the fire safety that society teaches us. Like, don't set fires, don't leave a stove unattended and more.

Thirdly, to fire setters lighting fires is normal whereas we consider fire setting to be strange and abnormal.

Finally, the last main difference between firesetters and non-fire setters are firesetters have a serious interest in fires. Think about your favourite hobby or job, like cooking, psychology, writing, going out with friends and that's how much fire setters LOVE fire.

Trajectory

Personally, I am always a fan of reading about research done by Gannon because she works at my University, not that I've ever met her, but I really like her research. Since in Forensic Psychology, I outline a great theory of hers and how it unites different parts of the research literature. And she's done the same thing here again.

Leading us to look at her's and her peers' Multi-trajectory theory of Adult Fire Setting (M-TTAF) by Gannon, O'ciardha, Doley and Alleyne (2012) that looks at why fire setting occurs. I know we've already looked at this to varying degrees, but this theory tells us how the fire setting behaviour starts, and what leads a person to become a fire setter.

Therefore, the theory proposes there are different trajectories that lead to fire setting. As well as each trajectory has its own antecedent, unique vulnerabilities to the firesetters and critical risk factors. Leading to the fire setting.

The trajectories are:

- Antisocial where the fire setter does their offending because of their antisocial behaviour and this links to the previous points mentioned in the chapter.
- Grievance where the fire setter starts setting the fires out of anger and they have a grievance against the target.
- Fire interest- here the person starts their fire setting because they have an interest in fire that they want to explore.
- Emotionally expressive and need for attention- this links into the previously mentioned points about some arsonists use their fires to get attention.
- Multiple-faceted- this trajectory includes a mixture of the other trajectories that interact together to cause the fire setting.

In my opinion, I do like this theory because it

unites a lot of the research already mentioned in the chapter, as it assumes multiple causes.

If you've read any of my other books, then you know how much I love research that looks at all the possible causes of a behaviour. Instead of trying to reduce it to one single cause. This is also known as holistic research.

Other Aspects of The Development of Fire-Setting Behaviour:

I know, I know this isn't a Developmental Psychology book but there are almost always childhood or developmental factors that can cause a behaviour to manifest. This is certainly true for firesetting behaviour.

Since the caregiver environment in childhood plays a role in arsonist development. Since as mentioned before if a parent has no interest in their child, this can lead the child to try and find other ways to get attention. Including fire setting.

Another factor is social learning where people learn by watching others. For instance, if a child watches their friends or adults set fires and get enjoyment from it. Then they would learn how to set fires and get enjoyment from it too.

One interesting factor that is involved in the development of fire setting is cultural factors that provide attitudes and beliefs about fire. This is an interesting point because, in western society, there is a restriction on children's learning about fire. Making it a scary, dangerous and forbidden thing that you must not play with. Of course, this deters the majority of the children from getting a serious interest in fire. However, this and other cultural factors can make playing with fire without their parents knowing an empowering experience. Then it could be argued this feeling of empowerment if the child feels powerless in their everyday life could lead to more fire setting because they want to feel empowered.

In addition, biological factors and/or temperament play a role since the feelings involved in fire setting are caused by neurochemical reactions.

Also, as previously touched upon psychological vulnerabilities are important to consider.

However, a more interesting factor or range of factors in fire setting development is the role of cognition. Since a child who sets fires tends to have an inappropriate interest and mental scripts. These scripts allow the person to know exactly how to set a fire.

Subsequently, some other cognitive factors include offences supporting thinking patterns. Like, setting fire to a building is harmless. As well as the person's emotional, self-regulation and communication issues can all have a role in the development of fire setting behaviour.

Finally, a behaviour can always start but unless there are maintaining factors then the behaviour will stop. This is why reinforcement is so important to maintaining fire setting behaviours. This can include sex, money, attention amongst others. I really recommend checking out Forensic Psychology for more information.

CONCLUSION

Over the course of this book, we've investigated property crimes, shoplifting, burglary and arson.

Personally, I really enjoyed researching and writing this book because theft, shoplifting and the other crimes spoken about are commonplace. This makes understanding the psychology behind these crimes even more important.

Since, this will allow us to build up the literature so practitioners can draw on this data and use it to help people, and hopefully reduce the chance of people committing these types of crimes.

Also, I really wanted to thank you as the reader for buying this book and supporting my work. I love Forensic Psychology and it was only because lots of people bought my main Forensic Psychology book. That I was able to share more information with you about this great area of psychology.

So, thank you for reading and I hope to see you in another book!

Or you can check out The Psychology World Podcast on your podcast app to learn a lot more about psychology!

BIBLIOGRAPHY

Howitt, D. (2018). Introduction to forensic and
criminal psychology. Essex, UK: Pearson. 6th edition.

Brown, J., Shell, Y. & Cole, T. (2015). Forensic
Psychology: Theory, research, policy and practice. 1st
edition

Wood, J. & Gannon, T.A. (2009). Public opinion and
criminal justice. Devon, UK: Willan Publishing.

Thank you for reading.

I hoped you enjoyed it.

If you want a FREE book and keep up to date about new books and project. Then please sign up for my newsletter at www.connorwhiteley.net/

Have a great day.

CHECK OUT THE PSYCHOLOGY WORLD PODCAST FOR MORE PSYCHOLOGY INFORMATION!

AVAILABLE ON ALL MAJOR PODCAST APPS.

About the author:

Connor Whiteley is the author of over 30 books in the sci-fi fantasy, nonfiction psychology and books for writer's genre and he is a Human Branding Speaker and Consultant.

He is a passionate Warhammer 40,000 reader, psychology student and author.

Who narrates his own audiobooks and he hosts The Psychology World Podcast.

All whilst studying Psychology at the University of Kent, England.

Also, he was a former Explorer Scout where he gave a speech to the Maltese President in August 2018 and he attended Prince Charles' 70th Birthday Party at Buckingham Palace in May 2018.

Plus, he is a self-confessed coffee lover!

Please follow me on:

Website: www.connorwhiteley.net

Twitter: @scifiwhiteley

Please leave on honest review as this helps with the discoverability of the book and I truly appreciate it.

Thank you for reading. I hope you've enjoyed it.

All books in 'An Introductory Series':

BIOLOGICAL PSYCHOLOGY 3RD EDITION

COGNITIVE PSYCHOLOGY 2ND EDITION

SOCIAL PSYCHOLOGY- 3RD EDITION

ABNORMAL PSYCHOLOGY 3RD EDITION

PSYCHOLOGY OF RELATIONSHIPS- 3RD EDITION

DEVELOPMENTAL PSYCHOLOGY 3RD EDITION

HEALTH PSYCHOLOGY

RESEARCH IN PSYCHOLOGY

A GUIDE TO MENTAL HEALTH AND TREATMENT AROUND THE WORLD- A GLOBAL LOOK AT DEPRESSION

FORENSIC PSYCHOLOGY

THE FORENSIC PSYCHOLOGY OF THEFT, BURGLARY AND OTHER RIMES AGAINST PROPERTY

CRIMINAL PROFILING: A FORENSIC PSYCHOLOGY GUIDE TO FBI PROFILING AND GEOGRAPHICAL AND STATISTICAL PROFILING.

CLINICAL PSYCHOLOGY

FORMULATION IN PSYCHOTHERAPY

Other books by Connor Whiteley:

WINTER'S DISSENSION

Companion guides:

BIOLOGICAL PSYCHOLOGY 2ND EDITION
WORKBOOK

COGNITIVE PSYCHOLOGY 2ND EDITION
WORKBOOK

SOCIOCULTURAL PSYCHOLOGY 2ND
EDITION WORKBOOK

ABNORMAL PSYCHOLOGY 2ND EDITION
WORKBOOK

PSYCHOLOGY OF HUMAN RELATIONSHIPS
2ND EDITION WORKBOOK

HEALTH PSYCHOLOGY WORKBOOK

FORENSIC PSYCHOLOGY WORKBOOK

Audiobooks by Connor Whiteley:

BIOLOGICAL PSYCHOLOGY

COGNITIVE PSYCHOLOGY

SOCIOCULTURAL PSYCHOLOGY

ABNORMAL PSYCHOLOGY

PSYCHOLOGY OF HUMAN RELATIONSHIPS

HEALTH PSYCHOLOGY

DEVELOPMENTAL PSYCHOLOGY

RESEARCH IN PSYCHOLOGY

FORENSIC PSYCHOLOGY

GARRO: GALAXY'S END

GARRO: RISE OF THE ORDER

GARRO: SHORT STORIES

GARRO: END TIMES

GARRO: COLLECTION

GARRO: HERESY

GARRO: FAITHLESS

GARRO: DESTROYER OF WORLDS

GARRO: COLLECTION BOOKS 4-6

GARRO: COLLECTION BOOKS 1-6

Business books:

TIME MANAGEMENT: A GUIDE FOR STUDENTS AND WORKERS

LEADERSHIP: WHAT MAKES A GOOD LEADER? A GUIDE FOR STUDENTS AND WORKERS.

BUSINESS SKILLS: HOW TO SURVIVE THE BUSINESS WORLD? A GUIDE FOR STUDENTS, EMPLOYEES AND EMPLOYERS.

BUSINESS COLLECTION

GET YOUR FREE BOOK AT: WWW.CONNORWHITELEY.NET